Liberation

Break Free from Your Own Chains and Live Better!

By

Debra Benowitz

Dedication

Great people are usually unaware of their greatness and I don't mean 'Mr. Buff' kissing his arm muscles. I mean those who impact others greatly. Most of the time they had no idea they've helped you until you let them know as it may have been unconsciously done or in action of simply who they are. So here it goes...

In dedication:

To my family; for making me so strong and generously accepting to others. It's been a long, winding and weird journey. Without your high expectations, I would not have so many accomplishments and become who I am today.

To Jacqueline Allen; for your 'specialness' and support throughout my life's journey and for clarifying I am not meant to be nor to do regular things. Maybe one day we will get that breakfast delivery started!

To my mentor, Mr. Ira Sterne; for giving me the start to a grand journey through the world of ethics and education. Your eccentricity, your rebelliousness against standardization and pure love and dedication to your students opened my eyes to a new world of understanding, which without, I may never have taken this enduring, yet exceptional path.

To my doctors; who used me as a disease exhibit for research and study and...

To Dr. Rathna S. Mallela; who displayed interest in me for research; *I'm sure there were other choices.* Your interest has enlightened me on the value of my circumstances and ability of insight. This enlightenment was the spark that led to the sharing of this great value, in effort to live free as who I am and to help others by giving them value and faith within their selves too.

Sections

Foreword

I woke up this morning and had an epiphany. I'm going to become a writer. I always write, always thought about it, but today I had the grandeur idea that I am going to do it as in publish and sell it. Here comes the anxiety. Others are going to read my thoughts? What if they don't like it? It is thought processes such as these as to why we don't follow through with our dreams or goals.

Uh Oh! Now paranoia; is this the grandeur idea they speak about when describing delusions?? It was on the symptoms list for chronic Epstein Barr virus; a diagnosis I am sort of dealing with as it is many times dealing me.

I was born with cystic lymphangioma and lymphangioma circum scriptum. It is such a rare disease that the spellings aren't even in the Microsoft Word dictionary. The first tumor I had removed was at 6 months old and the last, when I was 25. Hopefully that will be the end of the cystic, however, the scriptum stays put. It's sort of a really ugly rash on my hip. It's quite discomforting, yet it sucks more to explain it to people than it does to live with it, like with all ailments.

And to add, Celiac disease. As if I wasn't awkward enough, now I have to eat a specific diet. In the process of trying to figure out why I was and am feeling sick all the time, without energy and the desire to sleep endlessly, I was diagnosed with severe anxiety and depression caused by having too much trauma in my life. The sicknesses are apparently just additives. It would take me a novel or several to tell my life story and to explain the many details so let's just say it was far from picture perfect.

This is not the first time I have faced severe physical or mental ailments. However, it is somehow different this time. Even though I have more reason to give up at this point, I decided I had enough and it was either euthanasia or figuring out how to live with it and not just to live, but to live better!

I mean who ever heard of neutropenia? Ha! It's even in the Word dictionary and with all my medical knowledge, I didn't know they even tested for such a thing! Here come more diet restrictions. Bring it on!!

Okay, so back to the grand epiphany or delusion, whatever one desires to call it, I write about a lot of things from philosophy to poetry to bathroom reading books, etc. and I never went through any sort of process to try and publish, however, this idea came from a new perspective; in light of helping others, in the past, through coaching and philosophy, the constant look of surprise on the faces of people whose perceptions of me were always off and the interest many display in my many circumstances and myself gave me the idea, maybe my "*specialness*" could be helpful for everyone. Who knows? Maybe this is why I'm so "*special.*"

So, in the case you find anything in this book enlightening, amusing, touching, useful, life altering, etc. I have, in the essence, put to good use, my abilities or disabilities, however one chooses to label it.

Introduction

This book is not sappy, not artificial and not encyclopedic, but blunt. You're down and you don't want to be, otherwise you wouldn't have picked up this book. If you can't figure out why you are feeling down, that sucks even more. So here's the scoop. This book is not a pill. It is not your fairy godmother. There is no wand that is going to poof you better. Not in this book and not at all. Like everything in life it takes time and work to reach goals. This book is to help you get started on that path by understanding you, your environment, and what you can do. It will likely stay with you throughout your journey, however, at its' end, you won't need it anymore. You may not even want to look at it. In the meantime, you are going to need a pencil; a pencil because you may need to at some point erase or change some things. Therefore, you will also need an eraser. Last, you will need a research tool such as the internet or library. I did mention, you will be working to get to those goals.

My purpose is to help you help yourself. Without self-help there is no help. How you use this book and other resources to better your life is up to you. I can only tell you the sky is blue. If you don't go look for yourself you will never know. However, if you're color blind, you may need to build some concepts to "see the sky as blue" before you can understand why it is blue to others.

You You You

I could write research and statistics about sicknesses, depression and other mental ailments, but with the many medications and diagnoses out there, I think the point is well said. There are millions of people with issues, but the only person that matters right now is YOU!

Children, relationships, family, etc. will survive while you nurture yourself back to health. You are no good to them if you are not well anyway. There are just some things you need to come to terms with.

You can only control you. If you're not driving the car, you may cause the driver to have issues or direct him, but since you can't have full control over the vehicle from the passenger side, don't try to drive it. Likely, it will not turn out well for you or anyone in the vehicle. Now back to you!

There are endless reasons for mental ailments. Just about all of them extend from genetics, sicknesses or environment. However, since you can only control you, you can only change you! You do not have to live life feeling bad. In many cases we can change our lives drastically by changing our reactions to situations. This takes some learning and the digestion of several concepts. Also, there are many resources out there. Learn to research. YOU know YOU best! Doctors are very helpful in most cases, but we are not always able to explain correctly what we are feeling. This can cause many things to be overlooked in the doctor's office. For instance, a great guy told me about some bee goo that helped with Epstein Barr and it was the first time I had energy in over a year. I kept telling doctors I just don't feel good and have no energy. Boy, did they try a lot of things!!

There are many ideas you can look into that would suit your needs. The fact is, many people have similar symptoms, yet the same treatment does not work for all of them. For instance, vitamin C may be good for the immune system in all people, but some are allergic and others get severe migraines. These people need to find their 'vitamin C' based on their thoughts, their beliefs and physical well-being. What works for you? Of course, you can't answer this question just yet. You need some time, some research and some learning about you first.

Oh, "The Sayings!"

Ever notice when someone is down they have more need for sayings or phrases related to their issues? Sometimes you can note someone's issue by relating a song and/or phrase they are listening to. It makes us feel better knowing there is someone out there going through the same thing, feeling the same way or we are not inept alone.

(I personally enjoy philosophy and can't live a day without noticing a new saying or phrase. There is a moral to be learned in everything so you will notice many sayings throughout this book. Some are my own and others I've heard. The ones I've heard elsewhere are noted in the back of this book as to where I've heard them. Many sayings need more explanation or rewording to fit realism and some are so simple and sensible, yet so complex to follow.)

It's time to live more and think less. Not in the sense you should be unruly to others or in general. However, this is *easier said than done,* Right? Just live without wonder. It's like taking a test and changing your answers in the last few minutes of class. Second guessing usually bears wrong answers and it's because your first thought was based on your instinct. *(As you read this book, you may begin to find your instincts wiser than your thoughts.)*

Go into the sun even if you have to go fully covered. It is the vital organ of life and energy. We have constant worry about cancer and germs and are fed endless societal prescriptions from diets to do's and don'ts, what vitamins to take or not to take and medications, yet you are not cured and we are all still dying. We still haven't been able to stop time or control the deaths of so many, either by 'accident', born with disease, murder, etc. Time is like tomorrow. It is not guaranteed. Spending it feeling bad is not the way to go.

Things don't always go according to plan and this is some of our greatest let downs. *You can plan a pretty picnic but you can't predict the weather.* Let go. A plan is like tomorrow. It may never happen. You can't truly forecast the weather.

There's a chance of rain on Wednesday. Well, it's only Sunday and again, you are just a passenger and you don't have control over the car. You can't even reach the pedal. If the car goes in an unexpected direction, let things be. In the great upset of things not going your way or as expected, you're missing the unplanned.

We couldn't have planned it better! Ever hear that phrase? In another light, most of your life wasn't planned. YOU might not have been planned. There isn't some blue print set up of how things are supposed to turn out. Somehow they just do or in other words, *life will find a way.*

Things always happen for a reason, of course, but we never understand the reason at the time of occurrence. So, if you don't slit your wrist over that terrible relationship, you may find out why it happened years later or not, but this is quite the popular saying when something terrible happens or something good comes out of something not so good. Why? It's sort of like religion. It's helpful for us as we always need an answer to the question of WHY or HOW something so awful could have occurred AND if it was the grand PLAN of something or someone else, it is for some reason acceptable.

"The grass is greener on the other side?" NO! *"THE GRASS IS GREENER WHERE YOU WATER IT."* Stop thinking going to some far off place is going to save you from something. It's your own mind that needs changing. In the Caribbean they sell shirts that say, *"Same shit, different Island."* Even in 'paradise' they have issues. Now I'm going to burst your bubble if it hasn't already been done. There is no such thing as paradise. Paradise is a state of mind; not a state. If you have been stabbed more than once in your lifetime and can still smile and love life, you have succeeded. You are actually better off than the average person who has faced only 'minor' ailments. I marked minor as what is minor to one is major to another. One should never judge the understandings of another. We all see and take in the world differently. The A student crying over their first B seems like an infant to the F student. However, their environment, culture and surroundings are likely much different than the F student's, even though it is obvious the F student is dealing with much more severe ailments.

The More We Learn the Less We Know

At some point I'm assuming we got smart enough to ask the mighty question of where we came from. Why do we exist just to live and die? Without purpose what is the point of life? Religion, in many cultures, fulfilled the answer to such questions for thousands of years. There are forms of religion even in tribes un-integrated with civilization. What does this mean? We all, humans, feel the need to have a purpose. Without purpose, there is a void, which I will discuss later.

I personally don't find religion fulfilling which may be culturally reasonable for me. Not to say, I am religious or non-religious. In studying science, and the many creatures of the world, I would have to say the main purpose of life is to reproduce. Species display great thrive to live and spread their seed. Now that I understand this, I feel rather unimportant and purposeless. So, like the ancient folk, I ask the question as to why I am here because I need fulfillment as everyone does. What is the point of me?

The Empty Pie

The empty feeling or unknown desire is a void; a missing piece. Imagine cutting into an empty pie. As the whole thing caves in, like a person's chest, there is nothing, but emptiness.

What you just visualized is what depression feels like inside one's body. Yes, a mental disorder, but felt in the heart or chest area and stomach. This is likely where the idea of a broken heart comes from. Now we just need to pump you up with some yummy pie filling before you cave. First we have to figure out how and what kind best suits you!

Here's a scenario: You've spent months putting together a 1,000 piece jigsaw puzzle and the last piece is missing. Now you know why the dog was having trouble going to the bathroom the last couple of days. However, you intended on using it as a wall hanging since you worked so hard on it. You now feel like you've wasted all that time. You could hang it with the piece missing, but it will likely bother you, especially every time someone comes over and mentions the missing piece. In this case, you need to become a thoughtful artist. The missing piece is not coming back and there is no exact replacement. You could sulk about it OR, instead, you could discover a suitable alternative. You may have to try different things to get it right and it may never be perfect, as in, the original expected outcome, but that doesn't mean it won't be great. However, what you use to fill the piece or void is important as you want to be sure it won't further deteriorate the puzzle or *you*.

Brief History of Man

The study of man always sounded funny to me. I am an anthropology fanatic and hold a social science education degree and it still makes me laugh. In order to study early man, one must study animals...or fossils and tools. So, at one point, we were animalistic and acted from instinct rather than thought or moral. At a later point, we were nomadic. At this point, we still were doing things wisely. The food runs out, then you go where the food is. Duh!

Then, in a text by Jean Jacques Rousseau, a French philosopher, some sense came out of how man went from as he explained, 'good' to well, not good. After the agricultural revolution, way back when people figured out how to plant and domesticate animals, came the *ownership of property*. This eventually caused competition between men and, in the short, led to materialism, social stature, and more simply the desire for overabundance or unnecessary items to display who is better than whom.

Rousseau had a great point, as it has been the never ending battle of who is "king of the mountain" which you are unnecessarily caught up in. What do you need to survive?

List items in the boxes below:

Beyond these items everything is

a desire.

What is Causing You to Suffer?

Buddha describes all life as suffering which is caused by desire. He is not pessimistic in meaning or he doesn't mean life is generally awful, however, we must understand, usually, if there is suffering there is a cause or desire. If the suffering is continuous, there is something empowering this cause. Only you should have the ability to empower someone or something to cause you to suffer, because guess who is in control of you?

(*This is not to say if you're getting bamboo stuck under your fingernails you can control the pain unless you have become a great meditator. However, if you have been tortured, in any sense of the word, you do not deserve to spend the rest of your life in misery or any time period at all. It cannot be undone. Only your way of thinking can be. This may be a difficult concept to swallow, but give it some time.*)

When we see a person starving or hungry, especially in those horrifying donation commercials, we tend to naturally feel bad as we assume they are unhappy or suffering. However, if Donald Trump was in turmoil with himself, we would naturally feel the opposite as he 'has everything', yet he is unhappy. The fact is, anyone can have a void or feel depressed. Materials, including beauty, are no matter. Imagine filling a pie with home goods, beauty supplies or clothing. Eventually someone is going to cut into it and find out it's not what they were expecting; out go the materials as they didn't obtain the desired reaction and BAM! The pie is empty again. Instead, the pie needs to be filled with something realistic, yet suitable for you.

In the boxes on the following page, you are going to list what you feel or think is causing your unhappiness, issue, depression or void. If you don't know, it's okay, just leave it blank. You may figure it out on your path to wellness, through research or there literally may not be a cause other than chemical imbalance. Either way, you can fill it in later.

(Is there a possible cause for the chemical imbalance; something environmental or internal?)

Not knowing why you feel a certain way is difficult because there is nothing to start with. What do you change or try if you don't know what's wrong? Also, not understanding why you are feeling down can lead to deeper depression as you may feel you don't have the 'right' to feel this way.

What's Causing You to Feel Down?

List things in the box below YOU think are causing you to be unwell.

Unattainable desires can become relentless so ask yourself: *What about receiving this want is satisfying or is it?*

If you are having an issue or dealing with a particular situation, decide how serious it is or isn't.

Always remember to pick your battles. You can't fight everything so win the worst of them or should I say the best or most relieving?

Getting Organized; In the Mind

Being down or trying to begin when things are cluttered can be difficult. There are goals you want to reach, but may not know where or how to start. These things can put you at a halt as looking at the 'big picture' can be overbearing or intimidating. At first your mind may look something like this.

This is a rather confusing stairwell at first glance and can be difficult to figure out. How do you get to the top, you ask? Before asking that question, what is at the top? I mean, why bother if you have no purpose of reaching the top? So, first, you will need to think about where you want to go, where you would like to be, and/or how you would like to feel in the long-term or at the end of the staircase.

<u>List your long-term goals here:</u>

Now that you have figured out your long-term goals, you will need to figure out how or where to begin. For each long-term goal you will need to come up with the first step in the direction of that goal. You may need to do some researching and utilize various resources to find out what the first step is.

(For example, in an attempt to appeal a wrongful decision, I couldn't find a lawyer nearby who knew how to proceed. I went to the court and started randomly asking lawyers in the hallway if they've heard of it. Finally, on the elevator, a lawyer told me he never heard of it, but it sounded like a specific article and to check in the law library. By the end of the day I was on the road to completing the appeal.)

However, most things take time and one day is certainly not enough, but it is a beginning and many times the beginning is the most difficult step to take.

Below, list your short-term goals which will allow you to begin a path to meeting the long-term goals you listed earlier. One for each long-term goal is plenty. You can figure out the next step as you go along.

I can begin by:

Goal #	Step 1

You have now organized your mind and the staircase, simplified! You are ready to begin climbing! However, take notice; the person in the following picture has only one step in hand and only steps up one step at a time. Trying to take too many steps or over carrying may lead you back to the staircase of confusion or to become overwhelmed. Keep in mind you are only doing what is in your capabilities at this time. Try not to think past the short term goal you are working on until you are ready to move past it. Many times the second step is unknown until the first step has been reached or begun. In other words;

Don't reach beyond what you can see.

Everyone is an Addict

(No one gets out of this chapter without a diagnosis. So if you think you can skip this one, wait till after you've read it to decide.)

So many diagnoses, so little life!

Let's start off with everyone is an addict. YES! EVERYONE! No addict is better than another. Some just cause serious drama, pain, agony and can be threatening to others. Whatever you do that makes you happy is an addiction. Some choose drugs, others knitting. However, if you can control doing what makes you happy at appropriate times and when you have the equity to do so, it is then called a hobby or social activity. In meaning, it doesn't affect your life or those you care about negatively. Others want to be happy all the time!!! That's the complexity of addiction. If your addiction is shoes, the excitement of the new pair only lasts so long before you're out there getting another. When shoes are coming before the rent, it is then considered an addiction.

For some reason us humans like to decipher things differently or give titles to make one thing seem better than another. If you think habit sounds better than addiction, this is labeling at its' best. Addiction is seemingly such a negative word. However, you are born with two addictions; eating and mating. Eating will outweigh the need to mate, but keep in mind this is the part of the brain being tampered with when it comes to addiction, especially addiction with drug use. It is also called the pleasure part of the brain in simple terms. If you please it with heroin you're going to have a long road ahead of you. You have supplied your deepest need with false supply. In the same sense, with any addiction, you are filling your needs or void with false supply. When someone quits or tries to quit smoking cigarettes, usually, it will make them feel the need to eat almost endlessly. It's because this part of their brain is suddenly lacking substance and is in overload of desire to fulfill its greatest addiction; eating.

(Look up unusual addiction or addictions in general. See what you find. It may be amusing, interesting or quite enlightening.)

Types of serious addictions I've encountered; some sound silly, but the people with them were quite disturbed when without for more than a day or less. These addictions caused them to be in debt, overweight, unhealthy, in trouble with the law, lose jobs, lose family, relationships and/or friends and thrive less to move onto other things or take on great opportunities.

- Heroin
- Book Reading
- Shopping
- Going to the Gym
- Alcohol
- Working
- Cleaning
- Over Eating
- Collection of a specific item. (Will buy such item over paying rent.)
- Gambling
- Smoking
- Chalk eating
- Constant need of attention from others
- Video games and/or Watching Television
- Texting, talking or using any cellular or computer device. (*I call it the 5th appendage.*)
- Prescription Medication
- Obsession with own children

- Nail Biting to the point of blood and pain
- Writing – Thank goodness not my own. After completing a master's degree that should be called, "Masters of Arts Writing Essays", I can't believe I got myself to write, but I thought these ideas might help others. Oh, and another addiction...
- Helping others. Sometimes those who don't necessarily deserve it or doing it over your own well-being.

There are many more. However, I think you can diagnose your own "happiness". For instance, if you're getting your nails done with your kids running around the salon and there are creditors calling your phone, you need to assess what about having your nails done manically makes you happy. You are no better than an addict getting a fix! Oh and don't think because you're knitting till your fingers hurt or because you work out incessantly that you're better than the girl getting her nails done! If you miss a day at the gym and it causes you to be self-conscious and not have enough time for a friend... Buddy, you got issues too.

Below, list any activities you participate in that cause you or your loved ones grief. In the column next to it, describe what about this activity fulfills you:

(Remember not all activities disliked by others are necessarily a problematic situation. Be sure to decipher if it is causing negativity to your person as well. For instance, if you buy a lot of shoes, but pay your bills, you're boyfriend needs to stop complaining. If you are going broke over it or no longer have room to sleep because the shoes are taking over, it is a valid complaint. Some addictions, you may clearly need outside help with and they are a bit more obvious. For instance, simply ending drug use will not fix all of your problems. It is the start of fixing them. Most addictions began in a troubled situation and are likely filling some kind of void. Just stopping one thing without understanding why you do it, will likely lead you to return back to it or replace it with another addiction.)

Activity	Fulfillment

Personality Disorders

Psychology for me was learning there were scientific names for the things we already knew about each other. You know the kid who was always being devious, the crier, the perfectionist, the pleaser, etc.; there are actually scientific names for those people and us. I always thought it was more like the "Peanut Gang"; you just have one of every type. I personally believe if you don't have any type or symptom of a personality disorder you are inhuman and should possibly be studied.

From the Online Dictionary; Personality disorders are defined as, *"an enduring pattern of inner experience and behavior that <u>deviates</u> markedly <u>from</u> the <u>expectations</u> of the culture of the individual who exhibits it"*.

(Take note of the underlined words; deviates from expectations. I will discuss this in a later section.)

Research the list on the following page. Be sure to read through all of the symptoms of each and to use more than one resource. If you find you have a symptom, put a check next to the disorder. If you find you have all or most of the symptoms of any of the following disorders, circle it. You are not bound to the disorders in the list. Any ailment can be added to this list. For example, you can add ADHD, Alice in Wonderland Syndrome, Bipolar disorder or Epstein Barr virus, etc.

(How could they name a syndrome after a well-known "children's movie?" Are they insinuating Alice has issues too?!)

List of Many Personality Disorders:

I.	Antisocial
II.	Avoidant
III.	Borderline
IV.	Dependent
V.	Depressive
VI.	Histrionic
VII.	Masochistic
VIII.	Narcissistic
IX.	Obsessive-Compulsive
X.	Passive-Aggressive
XI.	Paranoid
XII.	Sadistic
XIII.	Schizoid
XIV.	Schizotypal
XV.	
XVI.	
XVII.	
XVIII.	
XIX.	
XX.	
XXI.	
XXII.	
XXIII.	

If you have checked any symptoms and feel it is something you want to change, you can put it on the following list.

If you've circled any of the above **disorders,** list it in column **one**. In column **two,** write the **symptoms** that pertain to you. (*Remember you must have several of the symptoms to fit into any category*.)

List of disorder and symptoms of disorders:

Disorder	Symptoms

Write the causes related to your situation below:

What external (environmental) or internal (possible genetics) situations are causing or caused your symptoms? For example, if you lie a lot, is there some underlying cause as to why you lie?

List five resources you can use that will help you understand and cope with this disorder; a doctor, a group, an online resource, book etc. If you're seeing a doctor or intend to make sure you bring your research with you. This will help them to help you.

Resource List:

How to cope will depend on the cause or causes. Hopefully you've discovered some resources and/or thought of some ideas to cope with any disorder you may have found.

<u>Write various ways of how you plan to cope below:</u>

Society Defines Us; Illness Caused by Environment

You can do anything; the land of the free; the streets are paved in gold. If this was true for everyone there wouldn't be minimum wage jobs, recession and a Yale graduate working at the BJ's around the corner. You are not Rockefeller. These are childhood fantasies spread by society except unlike finding out when you're young, like you would about the myth of Santa, you are suddenly thirty and depressed because you are not all you thought you were going to be. Yeah, you could be like Mike, but your chances are about as good as winning the lotto. Let go of the 'hoop dreams.' The majority of adults are unhappy. If you were told you are going to grow up to work every day, maybe have kids, be in an imperfect relationship and die, you wouldn't be so let down. More marriages would last, less money would be spent trying to be something or achieve something that is not you or unnecessary and most of all you would have spent your time working on realistic goals instead of trying to figure them out now.

What's worse than being let down for some reason, is not meeting expectations of society or others. Many teenagers or recent high school grads kill themselves over unachievable, undesirable or just plain over-bearing expectations.

At this point you likely are thinking I'm being pessimistic. The lesson here is, you are what are and if you're middle-aged, you likely are what you are going to be. Either accept it or go to great measures to be what you desire. *(If you just got the sudden urge to go back to your goals list, you should do so.)*

Stop trying to please others. Some can never be pleased and you can't please them all, but you can please yourself. If your happy working as a secretary at a doctor's office and it's making ends meet, smile, you have succeeded!

If you are a surgeon and you go to sleep every night wondering if this is all life has to offer you, you have some soul searching to do.

"Desire is the cause of all unhappiness." People who have reached the point of being able to afford all the materials they wish, men who may have all the women they want, or those who have seen the many places of the world have likely learned, it is not such things that make one happy. In this society, not having money or materials may make things worse. They are not the cause of unhappiness.

You are not:

- A statistic
- A case
- An outfit
- A title
- A name
- A person with...
- A race/ethnicity

- A gender
- A job
- An amount of money
- A person without...
- Etc.

You are merely human trying to make it in the environment you're in with the tools you were given at birth. Everyone has a different set, however, society sets standards on the type of set you should have and well, if yours is not up to expectations, you meet the guidelines to receive one of the millions of labels given to you by others. It's comparable to grading eggs. Many times their tool set is missing a few screws as well so don't let the negativity of others bring you down. Sometimes you will find they are missing their measuring tape and are unable to calculate how big the world actually is. In simple meaning, they have some learning to do too. I mean, what really makes one egg better than another? I'm going to have to research how they figure that one out!

Materialism is a grand issue in our society and it is most pressing on those who have not. What purpose is it serving? This goes back to the competition theory and showing off social stature. None of it will solve your problems nor make you a better person or better friends. Why has it become such an issue? Because we judge and are judged based on our visual or what we see first, however, plenty of people wear jogging suits yet they never exercise. Many times the things we like or find attractive about a person aren't necessarily real, however, without the deceit or materials, you or they would likely have never participated in the relationship or situation to further get to know each other.

In college I wrote a comparison essay on the plays, *The Importance of Being Earnest*, by Oscar Wilde and *Sure Thing*, by David Ives. They displayed a thorough view in quite differing ways on the social theme of relationships, and how they are based on deceit. There is no person excusable from this as we have all at some time or another played a role in such a relationship. We even tend to deceive ourselves when we want or hope something will go well to find reason to maintain the situation or make it seem ok.

"You can't get nobody being you, you need to send your representative."

34

In reason, all the glamour and glitter will eventually fade and when it does, do you like who you are or even recognize yourself? What about the person standing next to you? Materials may get you by for some time, but not through to the end. Your best friend is likely so because he or she knows you for you. The greatest relationships are those that are realistic. So, can you stop caring or un-condition yourself of beliefs set by society?

One of the most interesting phrases I've heard was from a woman in a movie who finally figures out her situation is what it is and there is nothing wrong with it. The eye-opener!!! Prince charming has come along and she lets him go because he is the 'IDEAL' prince charming, not HER prince charming.

> *"You're like a fine Italian suit and we're just not suit people."*

What suits you?

Societal causes of out casting, depression and anxiety as well as other mental ailments are the beliefs of what you ought to be. Think about it. What makes someone really feel bad or insecure? Societal beliefs, expectations or beliefs of others, what you should or shouldn't have or should or shouldn't be, based on those beliefs.

Deviate from expectations of one's culture or society defines personality disorders and therefore unmet expectations can cause us to feel down, inept or inadequate, desire unnecessary items, act or react inappropriately and more plainly cause illness or disorder as defined by society.

However, here's the low down. Society is sick and we are all a part of it. It's in magazines, newspapers, television, the radio, the schools, the justice system, your very own home, etc.

A movie called, "A Clock Work Orange" displays a telling view of this idea. However, for many it is difficult to watch and/or to understand the first time around so I will explain.

Alex is the leader of the Droogies, a heartless violent gang that rapes, murders and steals. He doesn't go to school, respect his mom or authority. His mom pays him little attention and the only form of authority in his life is a perverted probation officer who wishes to see him fail. Throughout the movie are displays of littered streets, sexually graphic pictures on the walls of peoples' homes and in public.

The point is, 'little Alex' lives in a society he simply acts out. When his Droogies turn on him and he goes to jail for murder, he volunteers to try a new treatment plan to get out of jail early. The treatment makes him sick to the point of dry heaving if he merely sees violence, sex or other unacceptable behaviors. When he is so called 'better' or a good citizen he is put back into society.

When Alex gets home he has been replaced by a boarder and seemingly forgotten about, ending up with no place to go. As he is walking down the sideway he sees his old Droogs who have become police officers. They beat him as he gets ill instead of defending himself as he is unable. He is also unable to look at the naked body of a woman.

Essentially, Alex cannot to survive in his sick society without being sick too. If we made a person in American Society upheave at every feature of what is considered socially unacceptable, the amount of contradiction we would have to rid of is inconceivable. This is quite confusing, especially for the young growing up.

Do you do what you are told or what you see? Many people are left on their own to sort it all out and in the gist of things, though some are lucky, get caught up in undesirable situations. You were likely left on your own because any guidance you may have had was coming from someone trying to sort it all out too OR they were unaware there was sorting to do.

In opposition, the point behind the movie, *"Fight Club"*, another difficult movie to watch, displayed the loss of feeling in a man who abided, without imperfection, by the ideals of society which causes him to grow a second personality. This personality acts out his inhibitions of natural man. Here, too, though displayed in various ways, it is depicted when he is 'himself', he has no feeling even when a woman tries to arouse him. Since the character, Jack, was held back for so long, the displayed inhibitions were highly over exaggerated, where if he was free all along, he likely wouldn't have acted out so drastically.

(People play the role of Jack all the time, even if it is a simple situation. Someone was upsetting another person for a long time until the person finally had enough. Instead of acting rationally, the person totally wigged, said everything, all in one sentence of a breath, they had been holding in for months along with additives and bad words. This person was completely sane up until this very moment and maybe still is although others may no longer think so.)

The fact is, we are civil animals; animals trying to conform to rules and regulations, many unfitting while keeping moral as this is what separates us from the animal kingdom, however, our society is not made up of the moral it preaches and attempts to put restraints on unbreakable human desires, feelings or needs while pressing upon us materials and desires we cannot use nor maintain.

It is these types of unattainable expectations which devour the mind and bring about the person you have become. Basically, you are your reaction to your environment and you are therefore labeled as such. Can you change this? Yes, but it takes a great deal of strength and understanding of others as you have been conditioned.

Conditioning is not like hypnosis, it is proven to work. We all know this because when a traffic light is red we stop and when it's green we go. The same sort of thing can be done to animals. Going back to early man, even he figured out, if you touch fire, you get burned and you touch fire no more.

Life situations are more complicated than staying away from fire or a stop light, but your instincts and conditioning work exactly the same. Can you un-train yourself? Yes, but you're going to chance being let down, burned OR the new term; *the unexpected*.

Not everyone or everything is red or green. There are obvious warning signs and when you see them you should slow down or step back from a situation and evaluate things. However, not every situation is going to come with a yellow light and this is when you're reaction to the negative situation will decipher your well-being.

Your other option is complete avoidance of any and all activity which could possibly bear a negative outcome. This includes all activities you may enjoy, however, *"On the path of avoidance you usually run right into what it is you are trying to avoid."* Therefore, abstinence from life will only work out for so long before life finds you or in other words, *"you can run but you can't hide."*

I heard a joke once similar to the story I'm about to tell which I changed around a bit. I wrote it and gave it to a good friend who had fallen into some pretty bad stuff. I hadn't seen him for a few years until I bumped into him one day and he still had the story. He kept it in his pocket as a reminder even when he couldn't follow the right path.

A religious man is standing on the roof of his house during a flood. The water is at his feet when a boat comes by. A man shouts from the boat to him, "Come aboard and I will take you to safety." The religious man says, "No, I pray to God every day and I believe he will save me" and the man on the boat moves on. As the flood waters rise up quickly they meet the religious man at his waistline when another boat appears. A man pleads from the boat, "Please come aboard and I will take you to safety." The religious man says, "No, I pray to God every day and he will save me" and the man on the second boat moves on. Now with the water at the religious man's chin, a third boat comes to him and a man begs, "Please come aboard and let me take you to safety before you drown!" The religious man says, "No! I pray to God every day and I KNOW he will save me!" The man on the third boat moves on and the religious man drowns.

Because the religious man was moral and prayed his entire life, he did go to heaven, and when he reached the Pearly

Gates, he said to God, "I don't understand, I was good and I prayed every day. Why did you let me die?"

God replies, "I tried to save you, I gave you three chances and you turned them all away."

The moral of the story is; every chance you get may be your last. Take opportunity when it is at your feet.

Communistic Specialism

We are all special... sounds communistic to me. If we are all special then no one is. Okay, so, we are all special in our own way. Then some people might find this prejudice because they don't like what is special about them. We are all different by fingerprint and DNA no matter how you want to put it. It is literally fascinating there is no being with the same print.

In watching a documentary on North Korea, I found most citizens find the activities of society they participate in daily life, the norm, as we do. There are some who complain as we do and wish for difference, however, an 8 year old girl made quite an intelligent observation about United States Society.

She said, *"In a place where they are allowed to be so different, they all try so hard to be the same"*, yet we badger them. Instead of trying so hard to fit in, we need to discover ourselves and accept ourselves as we are. The second step is to accept others for whom and what they are.

Most people who can't accept others, don't like themselves. Just know you can always trust someone for what they are. If J.D. usually does annoying things, we can expect he will do annoying things. This doesn't make him a bad person, just rather irritating sometimes. Others may find him amusing. One shouldn't make him feel bad about his 'special' personality. It's just who he is and others may like it, so we shall not complex him.

In discussing all wanting to be special, we should not compare ourselves to others. We never know what they are going through, how they think and the fact is you are not them. Some things work for people that will not work for you and vice versa. Do what works for you regardless of what others do. Not to say you shouldn't try new things. Of course, when things aren't working, trying new things and the ideas of others may be helpful.

Since you have to compare yourself to another to be labeled special, whether you are religious or not, the fact the Ten Commandments as well as other religious doctrine has been around for thousands of years, makes them rather notable.

The 10th commandment, in the essence, explains we should not desire what others have. There are several versions of the 10th Commandment, but only worded slightly different and all, in meaning, are exact. It may be some rather moral feeling person thought of it and others thought it was a good idea too and just couldn't word it much better than the guy before him.

Here, is King James' version of the 10th Commandment;

*"Thou shalt not covet thy neighbour's house, thou shalt not covet thy neighbour's wife, nor his manservant, nor his maidservant, nor his ox, nor his **ASS**, nor any thing that is thy neighbour's."*

Okay, so it is obvious many people understood it was wrong to desire something solely for the purpose another possesses it. Reasoning; usually when you want something someone else has, you tend to begin to dislike the person or peoples while at the same time making yourself feel bad over having not.

However, in the immaturity and stupidity of noticing such, I think since every other version I've seen uses donkey instead of the word ass, King James understood the importance of having a butt. He knew it would become something much more desirable than a donkey, so he replaced it to help along with the changing desires of time AND he was right because the current population often stares at other people or magazines and thinks to themselves, "I wish I had a butt like that!"

In other words, stop wanting the butts of others and start being appreciative of your own **ASS**!!!

What are You Good At?

People often want to try new things when they are feeling low. There is nothing worse than trying something new and finding out you suck at it when you are already down. *However, remember to mind those addictions. If you gamble and are homeless you are not good at it.*

Achievements can be anything you have accomplished. Many times we do not see or think of the things we've done as something great. Remember, if it was difficult and you completed it or have overcome it, it is an ACHIEVEMENT!

First list your achievements:

Now list what you are good at or what others have told you, you are good at. It can be anything, even making pancakes.

I am good at:

Research what others have done or what is out there in your field of goodness. For instance, if you're great at making pancakes, learn how to make them different ways or throw a brunch. Hey, you never know, it can turn into an annual event you may wish you never started, but it is a start and you could probably use some compliments right about now.

If you read this and thought who to invite or you would be upset if no one came, you have quite a fair argument. The people you keep company with are as important as your desires. If your friend J.D. is unreliable expect her to be unreliable. She probably loves you but can't get her own junk together. This is not someone you necessarily need to cut off, just trust them for what they are worth.

Getting Rid of Your Demons

When I say, 'demons' I'm describing people, situations or feelings that pull you down or keep you from rising up.

You are your worst enemy. It is obvious your own bad feelings are what cause you to feel bad, but you need to question where those feelings are coming from. Again, there is a cause. However, what many do not realize, is the type of energy you put out affects you as well. For example, if you are negative, angry, sad, hurtful, plainly in a bad mood etc. you put that energy or stress unto others. Though, I have taught many a lesson on how energy flows through people by using a closed circuit, you can try it simply by smiling at the next person you see, even if it's a complete stranger. The person is likely to smile back and may even smile at the next person he or she sees. If you give the next person you see an attitude, they are likely to throw it right back at you and then spread it to the next person. In a sense, the way you feel is similar to a highly contagious disease. For some reason bad feelings are much more infectious and more difficult to cure. Therefore, you need to think about what situations and/or people in your life are negative or pulling you back and CONTAIN THE INFECTION!!!

(*My daughter had a really mean bus driver who was always in a nasty mood. He yelled, screamed and wrote up the kids for almost anything, so I told her every day she gets on the bus to give the bus driver a great big, "Good morning!" with the brightest smile. She thought I had lost it, but guess what? One day the bus driver smiled back! It made her feel good too. I could tell by her excitement.*)

If you are dealing with a highly toxic situation or person, it's time dump it!!

List the situations in your life bearing any type of negativity in the boxes below:

(Even if it's over doing the dishes which at some point earlier you should have deciphered as not an issue, rather more of an agitation and you could let go of the steering wheel on this one. It's like a fight in the school yard compared to the Civil War.)

There are people, who bring down others without a reasonable purpose, though they may have some inner purpose, it is not out of love for you.

Be careful of those who say they do it because they love you. This is a bit deeper, very cold hearted and much more difficult to move away from. You may not even notice it occurring until you are deeply scarred. Either way, you need to assess the purpose this person has in your life.

If every year when you go to Grandma's house, your cousin goes out of his way to embarrass you and it ruins your holiday, don't go to the following event. Make other plans or plainly don't go. Who cares if they're mad? At least you won't be and just maybe the next time your cousin tries to embarrass you, someone will do something about it.

You do deserve to be protected by those who care for you and when you are not, it makes you wonder if they care at all.

You'll be surprised how free you feel once you deviate from the constant expectations of those around you which you don't enjoy living up to. You are likely to do it more and maybe become your own person.

(This idea works especially well for people who just can't say no.)

This is in no way limited to family and friends, however, but to people in general. Some people on your list of demons you may not necessarily have a relationship with in any way, other than their bringing you down. In this case, you need to assess what expectations of this person you feel the desire to meet which allows them to make you feel a certain way.

You are not to do this in a spiteful sense, but to simply shake off the hands grabbing at your back. It may even be a good idea to explain your letting go, before you do so, if it is someone close to you. This way, the person understands why they have lost you.

Remember, you can't change someone else, but you can change what you allow a person to affect in your life. Keep in mind, when someone is able to make you feel bad, it's likely because you are not sure if they are right and only you can decide that.

Let go of overbearing people or family members, those who only call only when they want something and those who have no true meaning in your life, yet wish to see you fail or hurt.

Relationships only work when both people get something desirable out of it otherwise the one coming up short handed is usually left very unhappy.

**List the people in your life you have any relations with.
In the column next to it describe what you get out of that
relationship that is positive for you:**

Person	Benefits of Relationship

If you came up with nothing in column B, then cross the person off. Now go to your 5th appendage (cell phone, computer, etc.) and press delete. See if anything in your life changes from letting the person go. In many cases you may gain some things, like more money in your bank account, less aggravation, and more time for the other people on the list; like the people who WILL show up to your pancake brunch. Oh, and by the way, these are the only people that matter. Most importantly, don't love something that can't love you back whether it is a shoe or a person!

After you've rid of the 'demons' in your life that are people, go back to the list of negative situations you were in and see how many you can cross off. If there are any left afterward, you will assess the negative situations the same as you did the people. When you set your goals, you will list ridding of that particular situation as one of them.

Getting Rid of the Fifth Appendage; Realism

How much time do you spend in the realistic world? You know the one behind your PC, magazine, phone screen, i-pod, radio, tablet, nook, book, television, video game, etc. I hope you don't think because you're past the age of realization you really have the ability to constantly decipher what's real and what's not.

How often have these items made you feel bad, caused you to desire something or filled a void momentarily? These technologies are not bad, they are rather entertaining and there is nothing wrong with getting lost in a book or movie or forgetting the world for a short time, however, the computer age has made it impossible to come back to reality.

From the radio in the car to these pocket size items, it has, in a sense, become an extra appendage, like an alien parasite; a foreign object (alien) that takes advantage of a person who gets nothing in return (parasite) AND just in case you need to know what an appendage is, it's like your arms and legs. Since you had 4 and now there is a parasitic foreign object stuck to you at all times, you now have 5, or more, depending on how many of these aliens have leached onto you AND it's stuck in there pretty good. Five musclemen couldn't pry it from you.

Here's an interesting take on things. Studies show looking at someone else's Facebook page is a super downer; looking at your own, big upper. Why? DER!! People only post positive things and paint perfect pictures of their life or they are that "nut job" you see posting details of getting broken up with or other private issue as if the virtual world is going to give them a hug. I mean, did you see the awful post and call the person to console them? You did, if you were their close friend or relative who already knew about it, to tell them you are coming over to give them a hug, they are losing it and to stop posting their private business to the world, many of whom wish to see them fail anyway.

Let it go!! Facebook makes you easy access and most of the people you are "friends" with, aren't your friends. Well, they are your friends, virtually, or in the new 'real' world created by the computer age. If you really could tell the difference you wouldn't feel down because everyone on Facebook seems like they are living it up way better than you. You may be 10, 30, or 55 and you just "thought what you saw on television was real", like a 2 year old asking if Barney can come over to play.

Profile pages such as Facebook are the finale of marriage and the new cause of suicide and don't post anything you wouldn't want on a college application or job resume. You are being checked on by schools, jobs, etc. You're giving out a free background check with an abundance of information not even the FEDS had access to, to a bunch of people who have no meaning in your life. At the same time, everyone, on any online program, where you have a profile of yourself, including dating sights, you are not being you and whoever is on there, is not being them! If they were, they too would seem like the nut job posting their personal business on the World Wide Web, hence, the www.

However, the great purpose behind ridding of the 5th appendage is, you can form a relationship with it, yet you can't live without it or stay away from it for more than a few hours and it is NOT real. If you have a smart phone, you are connected to the virtual world at every second of the day! You need to come back and spend some time in the real world where 'real' humans exist; not the ones seemingly meeting impossible expectations.

You are being taken advantage of. It's not a conspiracy. It's a multi-billion dollar industry and it obtains the ability to keep you busy 24 hours a day viewing or listening to the propaganda of American Society. You know the 'what you ought to be' and 'unreality' of other peoples' lives which help you to forget your own life or which causes you to be inappreciative of your own **ASS**.

"If you want to know the weather, just look outside."

52

I call PC screens windows….hum, wonder if that's where they came up with the program called windows? Anyway, I call them windows because instead of getting out and doing, we are just watching. More and more we are becoming the kid who sees the others outside playing, but is too scared to go out, so he just watches through the window day after day. Stop looking out the window and go outside. Life becomes much more exciting.

We are social beings and need to move away from virtual relationships and/or worlds. They lack intimacy, proper communication, realism, and restrain human interaction and natural behavior. Look away from your phone and see what's going on right in front of you.

In restaurants, everyone has their phone sitting on the table, staring at it incessantly as if it is going to do something magical or texting like the person on the other end couldn't have just come to dinner. You might as well have gone to dinner with your fifth appendage, whichever one is deeply inserted in you.

(I have been out dancing and my girlfriends are standing in the middle of the dance floor texting or worrying about a phone call or text or what was just posted on the virtual daily social, meanwhile they are already in a place with the people who give a damn about them, where they may have a chance of meeting other humans, in the flesh, who may eventually give a damn about them too!)

That thing in your hand doesn't have the ability to love you or care for you and you can't have much fun with it unless there is someone on the other end interacting. That someone could simply meet up with you or hang later when you and they could have real time conversation; the type displaying true reaction without the thought process of writing or being answered hours later when topics are no longer appropriate.

Speaking on the phone is a step up from texting, however, the most intimate and communicative form of communication and relations are in person. I could give a thousand examples, but this one is unforgettable.

(I was feeling down, so I called my friend to talk to her about it. She understands, and so, she was "listening." When I asked her what she thinks I should do, after venting for at least five minutes, she says, "Dude, I'm really sorry. I was in the middle of taking a crap and I didn't want to hang up because you sound really upset. I'll call you back in like five minutes.")

Then, I felt worse, but that is technology for you. Right, she could have not taken the phone call, but I, or anyone upset, may then feel ignored and become more upset. However, the appendage was just unable to communicate as the human on the other end was busy going potty.

If you're already down, staring at a blank phone screen all day can get so downing you eventually have to change the picture or ring tone to make it less depressing or more exciting. What about this virtual world keeps us so caught up?

I dare you to leave your cell phone at home. It's worse than forgetting your lunch. The extreme anxiety it causes as if you left the burner on and for what, the fear you might miss a call or text or the daily virtual social on your favorite profiling page. If missing a call or text from someone is worrisome as if it will cause damage to a relationship or person not to speak with you, they need to go in the relationship assessment section! Otherwise you can just return the messages when you get home.

Most people do not work or go to school because they enjoy it. They do it because they have to. Therefore, you should have something to look forward to when you get home instead of texting and talking while handling the immense load of things in front of you. Not only does it lack intimacy or true communication as you and they cannot fully listen and respond, especially through text messaging, it takes away from the part of your life you need and enjoy; that of socializing with others.

Life is moving too fast as it is and doing five things while communicating or socializing is impersonal and unhealthy as is being accessible 24 hours a day. All of these gadgets make it impossible for you to have true self time and to just plainly turn off the noise. Heaven forbid you miss a text or don't answer the phone all day. Next thing you know you have the weight of everyone on your shoulders pressing you to explain what happened. Just plainly wanting to relax is inexcusable.

Why are we so easily assessable anyway? The person/situation we can't stand at work or school or wherever should be disconnected when we're no longer there. People used to go on vacation to get away. They come home and want to tell me all about it and I say, "I know! You posted every second of it online and now we have nothing to talk about. Bet the computer was at least excited for you."

(On my best friend's 30th birthday I took her to her favorite event, VIP style, where you get to sit a few feet from the front and meet everyone. She was beside herself when she found out and was having the time of her life until her

boyfriend text her. He was ditching their plans after the show. She was so hurt she couldn't enjoy herself after the text and we ended up just leaving. What a better time she may have had if she didn't have a fifth appendage stuck to her that night.)

Slow down. We all should have something to look forward to when we get home such as appropriate socialization or drama, whichever it is.

If there is someone in the waiting room, try starting a conversation instead of staring at your extra appendage. Maybe you'll make a new friend or a crazy stalker; who knows, but at least, just maybe, you'll have a great story to tell when you get home!

Come out from behind the window and others will have to do so to meet you as well.

Even better, there are now phones you can converse with; make it call you master! I don't remember who came up with the idea, but the kids think it's hysterical. You can ask it where to dump a dead body and it will answer you, but if you ask it to marry you or if it's your friend, it usually says it'll get back to you later on that one. Interestingly, this type of conversation isn't much different from those of the fabricated human relationships generated by the computer age.

"People are forgetting how to be people! With these robotic gestures, how we cling to electronics; raise LCD screens to our faces at the instance of an impatient distraction."

Try giving out only your home phone number, if you still have one, and make yourself less available. You may be surprised at the stress you have left behind, depletion of feeling overwhelmed and the greater enjoyment of desirable activities.

Putting Yourself on the Pedestal

The world is how you view it. Where the glass is half full or half empty concept comes from. Are you optimistic, pessimistic and, I feel there is realistic, sometimes seemingly pessimistic, however, rather intuitive based on experiences. Take a gander at the cube below. It's a simple, square shaped, box-like object, yet very complex in nature. As you stare at point **A** decide whether you are looking at the inside or outside of the box.

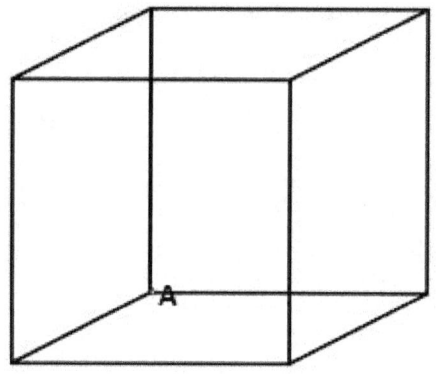

THE BOX IS NOT MOVING. THIS IS A FLAT PIECE OF PAPER SO MAKE A CHOICE! (Check one)

☐ Inside   ☐ Outside

If the outside of the cube is positive and inside is negative you can consciously choose to see the **A** inside or outside. It just takes some refocusing. This works with your view on your environment or world in a similar sense.

Whichever way you choose to see or react to your environment is what will cause it to be good or bad.

Everyone loses focus once in a while and its okay, but you have to remember to snap out of it. It's just an illusion.

Also, whatever you put on the pedestal is seemingly what you think is better than you or out of your reach and you need to *"think outside of the box."* If you want to be the gold medalist you're going to have to see yourself on the top pedestal. Nothing or no one is above or beyond you and you deserve to be up there! The **A** is out of the box! Remember, it wasn't easy for the gold winner to get to the top, so hardships and obstacles are a part of getting where you want to go.

Some say the more difficulties one faces, the greater the character the person will possess. This is an understatement! Oprah didn't become who she was by being fed with a silver spoon.

Why People do Messed up Things

Don't try to understand a crazy person or the crazy actions of a person. You may go crazy in the process. Just know everyone thinks differently and there are many levels and orders of thinking. This is an example I made up to explain to education trainees on how to accept the thinking level of a student:

(In teaching a pre-K class, the teacher asks the student's to tell her the different colors of apples. One student shouts, "Purple!" The teacher says, "Apples are not purple J.D." He then insists they are and the teacher and he begin to argue until J.D. says, "I will show you" and he goes and gets the art color book and sure enough, there is a purple apple in it. So, where to go from there? You can tell him real apples are not purple, but it is in his hand and he doesn't understand that concept yet. In this case the best thing to do is not to argue and to allow J.D. to have the understanding there are purple apples

as before he can see apples aren't purple he must concept build. In his world, apples are purple and he is not necessarily wrong. He just has some learning to do before he can comprehend what the teacher was asking him.)

There are many concepts we may not understand and this is more of the reason to be accepting and to keep an open mind. Knowing this should help to delay such a negative reaction or any at all. You can walk away and at most think to yourself how some people are just *so weird*.

It is the same idea for unusual situations. They do not always need to be deciphered. Don't try to make sense of everything. No one or nothing makes sense all the time. Neither do you and you are surrounded by an environment full of contradictions which is simply confusing, sometimes angering, hurtful etc. For instance, here's a silly one;

Do not text while driving; reasoning; it is dangerous to look at your phone and read while you are driving. Okay, so, that is obvious. It is not safe to you or others. However, you can spend an extra few bucks to get an encoded saying on your license plate. Have you ever tried to figure some of those out?! Try this one. (MW4KIDZ) It is impossible not to stare at the plate. All of a sudden you proudly shout it out cause you got it first, "Mom with 4 Kids!" as everyone in the car is screaming, "WATCH OUT!", as you look up and pump the breaks right before you hit the mom with 4 kids.

Hopefully you laughed at the stupidity as you understood the concept I was conveying. I have also inserted some license plate pictures I found online, considered funny or weird for fun. Because we all need to have fun and laugh too!

I don't think this was Reggie's original plan, but staying positive, he did get a lot of attention as now his plate is posted all over the internet.

(ASK REGGIE)

Thank goodness for the Letter I at the end and the ability to be half dyslexic or I would never have figured this one out!!

(PIMP)

This one is terribly ballsy. I know some people who would definitely crash over this! Imagine seeing this in your rearview and not double taking again and again. Go ahead. Put it in the mirror if you don't get it!

(FIGURE OUT AT OWN RISK)

Remember, I'm not a bad or deranged person. I found it on the internet!

The point is, you may never understand the WHY's or HOW's and life is too short to dwell on what occurred when you could spend time pondering on what CAN occur and begin to take steps in the direction of making great things happen or just plain things for the pessimistic realists.

In simplification, and finale, your choice is to live the way you are

OR

Learn to react differently to **disappointment**;

Defined as; saddening situation or let down or interchangeable with one of the following from the online thesaurus; failure of expectations or miscalculation, bad news, bitter pill, blow, blunder, bring down, bummer, bust, calamity, defeat, disaster, discouragement, downer, downfall, drag, dud, error, failure, false alarm, faux pas, fiasco, fizzle, flash in the pan, lemon, misfortune, mishap, mistake, obstacle, old one-two, setback, slip, washout, difficulty, dilemma, dire straits, distress, grief, headache, hindrance, hot water, inconvenience, mess, nuisance, pain, predicament, problem, struggle, torment, woe, etc.

OR

You will chance missing out on the antonyms, including but not limited to; boost, comfort, happiness, help, miracle, pleasure, relief, success, aid, allowance, assistance, enjoyment, indulgence, and...

LIBERATION!

Afterword

If there was any notable god, in our society, it is time and he's married to money. Therefore one could say money is the rib of time. The clock is ticking and we are moving at the speed of light to fill our days with as much as we can so we can enjoy what? And when?

The value of how you spend that time is priceless. No amount of money can buy it back and you deserve to spend it living better if not at its' best! In noting euthanasia at this book's beginning, I will end with it; as the idea behind it, is the quality of life. ***If there is no quality in life, are you considered living?***

My kid stood next to me the other day and was up to my nose. Last I remembered, he was at my hip. Then my other one comes home and I say to her, "your brother is so tall" and she's like, "Duhh!! MOM!!" So I asked her where she just came home from and she's says, "Um like School! Helloooo??" And I'm like, "How long have you been there and when did you start talking like that?! Why do you sound like a teenager?" Then she O-M-G's me and struts away.

Now I'm wondering if I was unconscious for like five years. Have I been so busy I didn't notice my son had grown a foot or two or that my daughter was in junior high?

There are many senses of busy. Yes, there is the physical form, which I was definitely caught up in, but there is the mental form as well. We obliterate our time caught up in thoughts and perceptions of things we many times cannot change, control nor understand.

Ever watch the movie, "Ground Hogs Day?" Bill Murray is stuck waking up to February 2nd day after day and at first he can't stand it until he figures out how to use it to his benefit. If something doesn't work for him one day in a situation, the next day he tries something else in that same situation until it works. Then he repeats what works.

Eventually, he gets everything he wants and there is a happy ending. Fortunately, for Bill, no one else remembers his mistakes except for him, however, we live in the real world and even if it takes us mistakes to get to where we want to be, eventually, we will learn what works for us and what doesn't, because whether you like it or not, time is leaving with or without you.

"The only regrets you'll have when you're dying is not making more of them."

Sayings

"There's a chance of rain on Wednesday."-Weather Channel
"Things always happen for a reason."-Life
"We couldn't have planned it better!"-Life
"Life will find a way." –**Jurassic Park,** the Movie
"The grass is greener on the other side?"-Life
"The grass is greener where you water it!"-Radio
"Desire is the cause of all unhappiness."-**Buddha**
"You can't get nobody being you. You need to send your representative."-**Chris Rock**
"You're like a fine Italian suit and we're just not suit people."-**Carolina**, the Movie
"Think outside the box."-Life
"On the path of avoidance you usually run into what it was you were trying to avoid."-**Kung Fu Panda**, the Movie
"You are your worst enemy."-Life
"The only regrets you'll have when you're dying is not making more of them."-**Bounty Hunter**, the Movie
"You can have a pretty picnic, but you can't prevent the weather."-**Outkast**, Song; "Miss Jackson"
"People are forgetting how to be people! With these robotic gestures, how we cling to electronics; raise LCD screens to our faces at the instance of an impatient distraction."- "Rewind Button", "Closed Doors and Opened Windows" By **Christopher Cajigas**
"You can run but you can't hide."-Life
"If you want to know the weather just look outside."-**My Dad**